Stop!

By Julie Haydon

Danger is all around you.

You must always
look after yourself.

Stop!

Do not run
across the road.

Cars and trucks go fast.
You may be run over.

Stop!

Do not ride a bike
without a helmet.

You may fall
and hurt your head.

Stop!

Do not jump into a pool.

The water may be too deep for you.

Stop!

Do not pat dogs
you see on the street.

Some dogs may bite.

Stop!

Do not sit or stand by a fire or heater.

You may get burned.

Stop!

Do not walk
on broken glass.

You may cut yourself.

You must always look out for danger.

This will help you stay safe.